POSITIVE PARENTING

TOOLS AND TACTICS TO SUPPORT
YOUR CHILD IN COMPETITION AND LIFE

COLLIN HENDERSON

@COLLINHENDERSON

COLLIN HENDERSON

WWW.THECOLLINHENDERSON.COM

INTRODUCTION

In my opinion, you could not design a better life teacher than sports. I recognize that I have a biased lens since I've been playing or coaching athletics for most of my life. But there are so many life lessons that sport creates, including dealing with failure and adversity, learning how to take instructions and implementing new learnings, practicing teamwork, and working hard to achieve a goal.

However, sometimes this essential life training is cut short because young student-athletes decide to quit. This opting out seems to occur at earlier and earlier ages possibly due to a growing need for instant gratification (Netflix, YouTube, SnapChat). This is tragic.

So why are so many young student-athletes throwing up their hands and saying, "I've had enough?"

Here's my two cents...

No matter the age, life can be stressful. From keeping up with the Joneses to the competitive nature of school, juggling work and sports, as well as the desire to belong—all of this can be extremely taxing emotionally.

Think back to your younger years. What sources of

stress did you deal with?

For children and teens, these younger years can be described as the best of times and worst of times. Youthful bodies are constantly changing, values and belief systems are not fully formed, and social pressures often arise during this stage of life.

All toddlers and young children look for validation from one source: a parent. "Mom, watch this!" Or, "Dad, did you see that?"

As children grow older, this social validation transitions to one's peer group. There is no pressure as strong as youthful peer pressure. Fitting in sometimes can even be a matter of life and death.

Though the importance of being cool among peers is at an all-time high during childhood and teen years, we still see athletes looking up into the stands with their arms and hands out after a bad call, mistake, or even success looking for parent approval.

Are there any players like that on your child's team? Is your child a bleacher peeker?

During these complex times, how can we help our kids not only perform better as students and athletes, but more importantly, be more self-actualized and happy as well? For me, it starts with understanding this simple point: Success and joy all begin with the right mindset.

Let me offer a quick mindset lesson to set the tone for this book.

We all have two voices inside our brain—*the Critic and the Creative.* Our creative voice is our true authentic self. This creative side of the brain is fully present in the moment. It doesn't judge, has effortless energy, and feels a deep sense of satisfaction while performing a task. This heightened state of consciousness is called being in a "flow state." Kind of like the energy and current flowing in a river. Young children who play, daydream, and pretend are often in this creative flow-like state. No judgment, just pure creativity.

As we age, this "open to all possibilities" mindset loses its frequency and power. That's where voices of fear, judgment, and the lies of perfection build. Another negative noise that we hear in our head is our inner critic. I also like to call this voice "The Judge." These voices try to sabotage our true self. This inner critic or judge locks us in performance jail because it is served by little mental minions that I call "Bad COPs." They Compare, worry about Opinions, and chase the lie of Perfection.

Unfortunately, sometimes parents enhance this critic inside their own child, especially during competitive endeavors like sports. I dealt with this as a student-athlete. My biggest hurdle of peak performance during that time was letting go of this pressure to meet the standards of my parents, especially my father.

My mom and dad loved me more than anything and supported me in all facets of life. They valued school, took my brother and me on vacations, and allowed me to flourish socially. There wasn't (and still isn't) anything they wouldn't do for us. For that I am grateful. On the athletic side, I went to all the camps, played on the best teams, and received the highest level of individual instruction. My dad was also a fantastic coach. Our teams flat-out won. This drive and success earned me a plethora of scholarship offers all around the country. My biggest fear, however, wasn't letting down my coaches, teammates, or team...but letting down my dad.

If we lost or I performed poorly, those car rides home were not very enjoyable.

Does this sound familiar?

Time has passed, and we have moved on. I have a great relationship with my parents, and I call my dad every-day. There were several years, though, where there was tension between us because I felt my dad's push for me to succeed as an athlete seemed to overshadow my self-efficacy in other parts of my life. During those years, most of my validation and self-worth came from my performance not as a person but as an athlete.

Most parents who create this similar push come from a place of love (just like my experience). They just want their child to succeed. From being on the receiving end of this approach, my goal is to offer a different perspective and possibly open some blind spots that you maybe did not realize how you are handling this crazy time of juggling many activities with your child, including athletics.

Being a parent with young children now, I am always reminded of how fast it goes. Let's make the best out of this amazing opportunity. For me, being married and a father is the most rewarding experience of all. Like most parents, our goal is to raise our young chil-dren into caring, competent, confident, and contributing adults for society.

The aim of this book is to give you the tools to do just that—to not only help your student-athlete enhance their performance in athletics and life, but most importantly, to improve one of the most important relationship you can have...the one with your child.

I've used some of this content when training high-profile athletes or sales professionals, but its relevance applies to children, especially young student-athletes, and that's why I'm including each of these subjects in the following chapters:

Chapter 1 - Whose Goal is It? (pg. 13)
Passion and drive cannot come from the external, but must come from within.

Chapter 2 - The BREATH Method: Five Simple Steps to Help Prime Your Child's Mindset (pg. 21)
A mindfulness system to help your athlete be more present in the moment, without judgment.

Chapter 3 - Mask of Masculinity (pg. 25)
Athletics and other competitive arenas are a breeding ground for ego and a destructive outdated ideals. In the end, love always wins.

Chapter 4 - Love to Win/Hate to Lose (pg. 37)
I offer a different way of measuring success.

Chapter 5 - Life is About Connection (pg. 43)
What brings us the most happiness? (Here's a hint: It's not statistics, money, and accolades)

Chapter 6 - Gratitude and Confidence (pg. 51)

I share methods to help instill a sense of gratitude and confidence within your child.

Chapter 7 - Five Killers of Peak Performance (pg. 59)
What you can do to prevent or help overcome common obstacles that hinder elite performance.

Chapter 8 - Help Your Child Deal with Stress (pg. 65)
Several techniques and strategies to help you quiet "Mr. Worry."

My intentions with this book are simple:
- To offer insights to support you and your child's relationship.
- To improve communication with your child to create a true team approach that fosters positivity and love.
- To provide you with proven strategies to help your child perform at their best.

As you obsorb the content from this book, here is a quote to think about from the late billionaire entrepreneur, Ray Kroc:

"When you are green you grow. When you are ripe, you rot."

I hope you are open to improve as a leader, parent, and coach, just like you expect your child or players to improve. Are you ready? It's time to get better.

CHAPTER 1

WHOSE GOAL IS IT?

When an athlete makes a mistake, you have ten seconds to make a choice: make yourself feel better or help them evolve...and it's all done by the words you choose to use. – Yogi Roth

How do you think your child would answer the following prompt and question without you in the room and knowing their answers were confidential?

- Finish this sentence: *Stress comes from...*

- What is the main source or origin of your fear or worry as an athlete?

As a high performance coach, I've asked these types of questions to many athletes over the years. During these discussions, an alarming theme emerged. As I broke down the responses, about 60 percent said that the main source of stress and fear does not come from the game, competition, or a coach...**but from a parent.**

This eye-opening discovery doesn't just relate to youth athletes. While working with a successful Major League Baseball player recently, he shared with me that one of his biggest struggles as a hitter comes when he plays in his hometown and in front of his friends and family. "That is when I've historically played my worst," he said. "Even if I was hot the series before."

I can relate. Being a successful two-sport athlete in the Pac-12 Conference, I had my own journey of balancing perfection and the push of pleasing my parents. This internal pressure would sometimes sabotage my own performance.

Being married now and a father of four children, I'm on a mission to change the culture of parenting in sports. My goal is to give parents the education and tools necessary to perform at their best, and improve their ability to support not only their child's performance but their relationship as well.

STRESS BY THE NUMBERS:

- Seventy percent of kids in the United States stop playing organized sports by the age of thirteen. *-National Alliance for Youth Sports*

- Anxiety is the number one form of mental illness in teens. *-National Institute of Mental Health*

- Eighty-five percent of college athletic trainers say performance anxiety negatively affects their student-athletes. *-NCAA.org*

You may think this does not relate to your son or daughter and that they are "fine," but most youth and teen athletes are not mentally or socially equipped to either speak up or address how they feel, especially during times of stress. According to Elizabeth Sowell, a professor of pediatrics, the human brain's white matter and prefrontal cortex, which helps with judgment and dealing with emotions, is not fully formed until after the teenage and young adult years *(Nature Neuroscience, 2003)*.

POSSIBLE SOURCES OF STRESS:

Self-Worth: Many student-athletes receive their self-worth and validation at an early age from feedback that is tied to their performance. Positive psychologist Heidi Grant calls this a *"Be Good Mindset,"* in which these performers believe that they need to perform "good" in order to be a good person.

Often, the ratio of positive feedback to negative feedback is off-kiltered to be more negative than positive. (Side note: Research suggests the ratio should be at least five to one positive to negative...what is your ratio?). The unrealistic burden of playing to be perfect sets in. Thus, like the concept of Pavlov's Dog, many children associate pain and shame with performing. When this experience hits a tipping point, they opt out. (How would you like being painfully critiqued after every day at work?)

It's Not fun: Specialization in youth sports, eagerness to be on the highest profile team, and pressure to earn a college scholarship are at an all-time high. Though the intention might come from a place of love, some young athletes are being treated like professionals with hectic training, practice, and game schedules. This grind and emphasis on outcomes often creates a pressure that takes away the natural fun of the game.

Ego: Some parents live vicariously through their chil-

17

dren. They receive their validation as parents by how well their children play, what teams they play on, and what attention and notoriety this generates. This correlation of performance tied to parenting creates an unhealthy sense of self for the parent, thus adding misguided pressure to the child (most often without the parent even knowing it). What is more important to you: your child's athletic performance or a healthy relationship?

So what can you do? Below are four tips to lower stress, improve performance, and increase your child's love of the game.

Let Them Fail: Many parents try to save their children from failure. This intention has merit, but it might be doing the child a disservice. According to performance psychologist Angela Duckworth, one of the best predictors of long-term human performance is what she calls "grit." Grit means having both passion and perseverance (emphasis on perseverance). Getting a prize for just showing up teaches nothing. Failing forward is how we grow. Learning how to be resilient and overcome adversity will help your child as an athlete and in the rigors of life.

Praise Effort and Attitude: Many coaches and parents praise winning outcomes only. This approach develops what Stanford professor Carol Dweck calls a "fixed mindset." Someone with a fixed mindset believes skill is fixed, avoids challenges, and feels they must prove him- or herself, which often undermines performance. To avoid this mindset, instead encourage your athlete to operate with a "growth mindset," focusing mainly on improvement and giving maximum effort. Also, look to reward and praise behavior that demonstrates unselfishness and teamwork. We can never control wins and losses, but we can control our effort, attitude, and how we treat others. Make these concepts the cornerstone of judging performance.

Balance: Encourage and support your child in activities outside of a single sport. Give attention and praise for effort in scholastics, music, and other productive extracurricular activities, as well as having good manners and helping others as much, if not more, than praise for athletics. This will foster a more balanced sense of self-worth and naturally lower stress during competition. (Also, here's a hint: Coaches at the higher levels love players with multiple sport backgrounds.)

Just Play and Have Fun: Children have amazing imaginations. Encourage creativity and playfulness by allowing them to be kids. A must for lasting success (in any field) is a deep passion and drive. Allow your child to develop a love of the game by letting competition be just that—a game (and not life or death). Fear of failure kills creativity. If their drive only comes from you, it will not last, and they will eventually quit. Allow them the gift of taking ownership of their own passion. Multiple reports show that creativity is the most desirable skill in the workplace. Let your child have the autonomy and freedom to just play, and let their creativity build and grow.

TWO QUESTIONS:

1. *Whose goal is it—is it your goal or your child's goal to be an elite athlete?*

2. *How long does it take your child to become a regular kid after the game is over?*

19

If you think it might be your goal, or it takes a long time for your child to switch back to being their playful, youthful self after competition, below are possible questions to help spark a healthy performance dialogue:

Are you having fun?

Why do you play?

What do you love about the game?

What makes you nervous when you play or practice?

When would you like me to talk to you—before or after a game? (I'm sorry parents, "during" is not an option.)

According to Bruce E. Brown and Rob Miller of Proactive Coaching LLC, from more than three decades of research, when college athletes were asked what their parents said that made them feel great and amplified their joy during and after a game, their overwhelming response was:

"I LOVE TO WATCH YOU PLAY."

This might be the most important advice to remember the next time you greet your child after a game and begin the drive home. This approach will not only improve your child's performance, but also your performance as a parent. Instead of doing a psychoanalysis on the game, just say these six words: "I love to watch you play," and watch how it takes your child's love of competition to the next level, and more importantly, helps him or her feel better as well.

Having a supportive and trusting relationship with your child is the best win of all.

CHAPTER 2

THE BREATH METHOD: FIVE SIMPLE STEPS TO HELP PRIME YOUR CHILD'S MINDSET

Practicing mindfulness and visualization have been proven to be a cornerstone of peak performance. Many young athletes are missing out on this technique because of a lack of emphasis, training, and consistent implementation.

Based on feedback from coaches and players, my guided visualization sessions (like this one below) have been some of the most impactful tools to aid performance.

To help you expose your child to a mindfulness system, here is a five-step pre-game exercise that you can do with your child at home or during the car drive to the game. This simple technique will help prime their mindset (and yours too), so they can be in a more relaxed and focused state (this only takes three to five minutes to do). I call this the "BREATH Method."

B – BREATHE: Ask your athlete to close their eyes, focus on their breath, and to breathe in through their nose and out through their mouth. If you'd like, have them count to five during each inhale and to five again

23

during the exhale (controlled breathing helps lower the stress hormone cortisol). After at least five deep breaths, invite them to go back to a normal breathing rhythm pattern.

R – RESET: Have them come up with a "reset" word that they can use to keep their mind in the game during down time, moments of stress, or when they fail (examples include: "believe," "confident," or "release"). Have them say their reset word to themselves in-between each breath or during the exhale. Example: Inhale...one...two...three...four...five..."Believe"... *exhale*...one...two...three...four...five. Do this exercise at least five times.

E – EXIT: Invite them to exit any and all thought, doubt, and negative energy, and simply focus on their breath and/or reset word. When an errant thought pops into their head (that's OK), encourage them to come back to their breath and reset word (this is taking a mental rep to strengthen their brain, much like curls for making our biceps stronger). Have them do a body scan and exit any tension and tightness as well.

A – AFFIRMATION: Once they have taken a minute or two to focus on their breath and reset word, have them identify a goal for the practice or game. Encourage them to use their imagination and visualize this goal as if it is already done (with as many senses as possible—sight, sound, touch, feeling, etc.). This will help create what sports psychologist Michael Gervais calls a "mental groove" or a neuropathway in the brain that the body and subconscious mind will later follow (this is also called "neuroplasticity," in which we can reshape our own brains). Make this connection even stronger by encouraging them to give themselves a few affirming statements of positive self-talk, like, "I can do this," "I"m worthy of greatness," "I've put in the work and I'm ready to go." Many top performing athletes, musicians, military, and business professionals use visualization and self-affirming techniques like this as a tool to reduce stress and improve clarity.

TH – THANKFUL: Lastly, invite your athlete to take a moment and think about what they are grateful for and what makes them happy. I call this a gratitude checklist (examples: faith, family, health, friends, experiences, etc.). Gratitude has been clinically proven to reduce stress by as much as 28 percent and create an optimistic and positive mindset (according to Dr. Robert Emmons of the University of California-Davis). Have your athlete learn to exchange expectation with appreciation.

This method will be of most impact if done consistently. Having a daily ritual of visualizing and activating the calming power of mindfulness will help you too. For your child, these principles will not only improve performance in athletics, but in school, and all areas of life.

CHAPTER 3

MASK OF MASCULINITY

Saying "I love you" to another dude or teammate is for the soft and weak.

This lie about love is one of the many "masks of masculinity," and I used to agree.

Being a coach's son and the younger of two boys, I grew up thinking that being a man (especially an athlete) was all about being tough. Real men don't cry, we don't show weakness, and the strongest are like Superman—made of steel and feel no pain.

I used to never say the words "I love you" to anyone, especially not a teammate. Even though my freshman roommate Matt Kegel (Havre, Montana's finest) told me "I love you" most nights before we went to bed in our tiny little dorm room, I oftentimes left him hanging. My insecurities, immaturity, and lack of hearing that from another guy kind of rattled me. Thus, I wouldn't reciprocate.

Matt and I were different, but similar in a lot of ways. He loved football, he loved life, and he loved people. You can learn a lot from a free-spirited Montana cowboy.

27

After Matt's many "I love yous, " I would feel uncomfortable.

That's weird, I would say to myself.

I was like many young misguided athletes, caught up in holding up a macho image. By not saying "I love you" back, I was keeping intact the mirage of my manhood. Sometimes, I'd steal a line from the movie Ghost, though, and say, "Ditto."

That was the best I could do.

I remember playing the University of Hawaii on the road my freshman year at Washington State University. It was the final football game of a rough season, and I was one of only three true freshman to start that season. One of the other three was Seahawks legend and Pro Bowler, Marcus Trufaunt. Marcus had just made an interception to close out a tight game in front of a hostile crowd.

I remember being so pumped in the heat of battle that I hugged him and said, "I love you, bro!"

I totally acted out of character but was caught up in the moment. I was playing with turf toe and bruised ribs that day. We had only two wins prior to that game and needed a momentum boost for the off-season.

It felt a little awkward saying it and even more awkward when he didn't say it back. *I'm never doing that again,* I thought.

Saying "I love you," is for girls and gays, not real men,

tough athletes, and coaches—that's the old mask of masculinity in me talking. This misogynistic and homophobic thought process unfortunately is still all too common in male and sometimes female team sports.

It's taken many years of study, self-reflection, and learning from successful mentors to understand that love is everything, no matter one's title, gender, or orientation.

I often see young people (especially guys) who haven't established their core values yet make immature remarks about love. Either they misuse it to gain an advance with women or never use it at all—especially with men, friends, or teammates. Often it's not their fault. Prominent male figures in their life and society have modeled this behavior.

Masculinity can be masked by ego, self-interest, insecurity, and the narcissistic adage that image is everything.

Gotta look cool. Gotta be hard. Gotta fit in. Gotta look tough.

Many "tough athletes" think showing vulnerability is showing weakness, especially in team settings. Who can blame them? They've seen "real leaders" yell, demean, and put down others. These leaders don't say "I love you," they're too busy being tough and focusing on kicking ass.

I argue the opposite. Being vulnerable is a sign of strength. You can have goals and grace. You can show love and hold people accountable.

During a 2016 match-up with the Arizona Cardinals, Seattle Seahawks place kicker Steven Hauschka missed a key fourth quarter field-goal attempt. A reporter asked Head Coach Pete Carroll what he thought about the crucial miss.

Carroll responded by saying, "I love him. He's our guy," regarding Hauschka.

Cardinals Head Coach Bruce Arians sang a much more familiar masculine tune. When asked about his kicker, who missed a late game-winning field goal as well, Arians said in disgust, "He's paid to make that."

Egocentric leadership is all around. We are living in an epidemic of misplaced masculinity. Bullying seems to be at an all-time high. Selfishness is everywhere. Entitlement is through the roof. Teams, schools, and organizations all have these types of people. I call them "energy takers," taking positive energy away from others. The many social media platforms are a feeding ground for energy takers.

There are many trolls out there that get some sort of enjoyment out of sucking energy from other people by posting disrespectful comments. These put-downs, in my opinion, often come from a place of insecurity.

Energy takers come in all ages, shapes, and sizes—ranging from your kids' teammates to fellow parents and even coaches. These individuals have no regard for others. They probably don't even realize how their selfish actions affect the larger group. They might claim to be all about "team," but their ignorant comments, posts, and even body language show otherwise. They blame, complain, and shame. These actions might actually be a cry for help.

Instead of being an energy taker, be an "energy maker," and encourage your child to be an energy maker, also—someone who uplifts, supports, helps, and cares for others. The world could use more energy makers and fewer energy takers.

Can you think of any energy takers in your life or in your child's life (work, family, team, school, etc.)?

I had the pleasure of working with a local top-ranked high school baseball team on mindset training, synergy, and culture a few years ago. As they began the post-season, I made a poster that I hoped would inspire unselfishness, sacrifice, and most importantly, love.

"FAMILY," it read, meaning:

F - FORGET
A - ABOUT
M - ME
I
L - LOVE
Y - YOU

When I posted this on my Instagram, an energy taker that I didn't know posted a comment saying, "This is soft. The only banners being used should be championship banners."

Wow. Energy taking at its finest. Unfortunately, this troll made a rash judgment without any context or being there to hear a few stories I shared to anchor the message on the power of love.

First, I shared an example about how a woman in her 50s had the strength to lift a car four inches off the ground to save her son who was stuck under a car.

The point: The LOVE of another can give you superhuman STRENGTH.

The second example I shared was a video of Clemson University's head football coach Dabo Swinney's post game interview after upsetting University of Alabama in the final seconds of the 2016 national championship game.

A reporter asked how the team came back and won.

Swinney said (and I'm paraphrasing here), "We won because of love. Love has been my word all year. I told them, I don't know how we are gonna do it, but if we love each other, we'll win."

The point: LOVE for your team, coaches, and program gives you FAITH.

The final example I shared was about Michael Jordan's love of the game of basketball. As a rookie, he made sure his agent and the Chicago Bulls inserted a "For the Love of the Game" clause in his contract. This clause meant he could play basketball in the off-season wherever and with whomever he wanted. Many teams put off-season regulations on their superstars, but Jordan wouldn't have it.

One of the reasons why Michael Jordan is the greatest of all time is because of his deep passion for the game of basketball. Similar to other greats like Tom Brady, Sue Bird, and Derek Jeter, these athletes don't play for money or for the accolades, but because of a love affair with their sport.

The point: Talent alone won't get you there, LOVE and PASSION create the pathway to greatness.

Trust me, I am all about winning. I'm all about getting after it and competing your ass off. I'm all about being a bulldog and hitting 'em in the mouth—all under the rules of play, of course. However, I'm just trying to shift the common masculine paradigm on how you get there.

It really boils down to this point: ***Relationships create championships.***

Relationships with others (family, friends, and teammates) are the most impactful part of being alive—not just winning.

Ask many athletes who are done playing, and they will tell you the biggest thing they miss about being a student-athlete or pro is the relationships, the time spent in the locker room, and being with their teammates—not the actual game.

In the end, you CAN'T control the number of banners, titles, and championships your kids obtain. However, you CAN control the depth and meaning of your relationships with them and encourage them to do the same, in their athletics, work, school, and life in general. A loving relationship is the ultimate championship.

33

If they love their teammates, team, and the process more than the ring, I believe they'll increase the likelihood of getting the ring, especially if everyone on their squad is on the same page.

Call me soft or Charmin, but that is the legacy I'm leaving as a husband, father, leader, and coach...a legacy of love—a love for myself, others, and to pursuing one's passion.

When football great Troy Aikman won his first Super Bowl, he found himself in his hotel room crying his eyes out. He asked himself, *Is this it?* He got the 'ship, but he wasn't satisfied...it wasn't enough. People change your life more then events do.

What is achievement if you have no one to share it with or if that is the only thing you play for? Also, if you judge your value as a person on wins and losses alone (as an athlete, salesman, coach, teacher, or whatever profession you are in), you are setting up yourself for constantly feeling unfulfilled—a trap I used to put myself in often.

We can't control specific outcomes. However, we can control our commitments.

Here's an exercise I did with the baseball team I mentioned earlier.

I first had the athletes write down their goal for the post-season. Almost everyone wrote down they wanted to win a state title. I had them tear up their original goal. Some were a little confused, but I explained, "Every team in this playoff has that same goal: to win a championship."

I told them that we can't control what happens at the end of this tournament. However, what we can control is our commitment to ourselves and our team.

I gave them a new sheet of paper and had them write down one commitment for the post-season. I had a few of the players share their commitment. It was very inspiring. Their focus shifted from all outcome-based to more effort- and attitude-based goals. The entire team then wrote their one commitment on the team banner that read *"FAMILY: Forget About Me I Love You."*

Commitments are more powerful than goals.

I felt this exercise would help narrow their focus, lower their anxieties, and channel their concentration on what really mattered. I challenged them to make this their only goal for the post-season: Focus on family, love, and their commitment.

I'm totally aware that this approach isn't for everyone. It's not the only way to win. But in my years of high-level competition in athletics and in the corporate world, LOVE is my vision and what I value most. LOVE is how I lead.

This focus and strategy worked for this specific team, too. By focusing on FAMILY and LOVE, this team won the state title.

My challenge to you is this: Reevaluate your understanding of the word love. Reassess your commitments to yourself, your family, others, and in pursuing your passion. As a parent or a coach, help your athletes evaluate and assess their understanding of love and

35

their commitments

Try to live life by this creed: *Let love rule.*

Jesus taught us, "These three will last forever: faith, hope, and love, but the greatest of all is **love**" (1 Cor 13:13).

The Beatles sang, "All you need is **love**. **Love** is all you need."

And again, coach Dabo Swinney's 2016 "word of the year" that guided Clemson to the national champion-ship was "**love**."

If it worked for Jesus, the Beatles, and Dabo, love just might work for you, your family, and your child's team.

Parents, don't forget to say "I love you" daily to your child—especially after a game, regardless of how they play.

Google conducted a study that showed "psychological safety" was the most important employee need at their company. Give your child the mental and emotional safety they crave in order to be comfortable in their own skin and feel valued regardless of outcomes. This will improve performance, opportunities for growth, and their ability to have fun.

When you unveil the mask of masculinity, and remove its insecure intentions, what you'll find is every living creature—even a macho athlete—needs love. And the best way I've learned over the years to receive love is to give it...even if you don't get the instant gratification of hearing, "I love you" back.

And for the record, Matt...I LOVE YOU!

CHAPTER 4

LOVE TO WIN/HATE TO LOSE

Answer these questions:

Do you love to win or hate to lose?

Does your child love to win or hate to lose?

During an interview several years ago, I was asked that question.

Interesting query, I internalized while I frantically tried to process this simple yet complex question.

I responded by saying, "Both. I love to win and I hate to lose."

The hiring manager challenged my answer and said, "You can't chose both, you have to pick one."

"Well, I suppose I hate to lose then, if I have to pick," I replied.

Let me preface that this was one of the worst interviews I've ever had. The hiring manager was one of the biggest jerks I've ever come across in an interview setting. He was hardcore, never smiled, challenged every single response I gave, and I let him rattle me.

He asked me if I was a rule follower. I said, "Yes."

He then asked quickly, "Well do you ever speed?"

I said, "Sometimes I go above the speed limit, I guess."

He said, "So then you are a liar; you do break the rules."

Cray-cray, right?!

But back to the question of whether you love to win or hate to lose. The positive thing about this horrific interview was it exposed me to a really beautiful question that challenges one's core values, motivation, and fundamental belief system. As a sales trainer and performance coach, I often use this question to explore a new hire's or athlete's paradigm and approach to competition. Most often, these new hires and athletes say "both." A close second is "I hate to lose."

Hating to lose is the dogma that has been ingrained in most high-achievers, go-getters, type As, athletes, and sales people all over the world.

Enrollment in select sports, advanced placement programs, and special clubs is at an all-time high for children and the ages are getting younger and younger. Personally, the idea that winning is the only option was implanted in my psyche early on from playing select sports at a young age. Many, like me, receive self-worth and develop identity based on wins and losses.

For three of my first four years in medical sales, I received a phone call informing me whether I was able to keep my job or not due to downsizing and lay-offs. Luckily, my sales performance was always good enough to stay employed. Winning and losing is often a matter of receiving a paycheck or not. This is true, but as I've become older and wiser, I feel like many of us are missing the point.

There is another group of parents and individuals that believe everyone deserves a medal, a golden star, and a trophy for simply participating. "We don't want to hurt anyone's feelings," they say. I unequivocally do not fall into that category or agree with this set of beliefs. I believe this is a huge problem that manifests entitlement, complacency, and narcissism. In life, sometimes you win and sometimes you lose. You get the girl, or you don't. You land the job, or they offer it to someone else. You get accepted into the college of your dreams, or your application is denied.

The point I'm trying to make is that failure is a key component of one's development. Two very different individuals, but visionaries in their own unique way—Tupac Shakur and Nelson Mandela—are both credited in saying the quote, "I never lose. I either win or I learn."

So many focus on the outcome instead of the process or growth. If we spend more time channeling our energy in our preparation, attitude, focus, and effort, the outcome is irrelevant. Growth, knowledge, stretching oneself, and improvement should be the emphasis. If you look at goal attainment this way, trust me, the wins will come.

Seek PROGRESS, not perfection...for you and your child.

When you or your child works hard, gives it all they got, and comes up short, there's nothing wrong with that. Obsessing over perfection will paralyze your child's performance. This approach of looking at outcomes from a different perspective might actually help people win more.

Being clutch is doing what you can normally do when it matters most. Being able to lay your head down at night in peace whether you win OR lose, because you are judging yourself (or your child) on a different set of criteria versus the W or L column, I think is the only way to live and perform at your (or their) best.

Personally, I can live with losing if I'm judging myself on my preparation, being present in the moment, and leaving no ammo left (meaning I spilled my guts going as hard and as intense as I could, with a purpose, passion, and a plan). The next step is to evaluate where I fell short, adjust, improve, and try again.

Are you parenting that way?

Do you praise outcomes or growth and effort?

Many of you have viewed losing the same way I did for most of my life. You give it all the power. This thought process forces people to miss the five-foot putt, strike out, or choke when they have to perform in front of their manager or a really important client. When the fear of losing is absent, and you shift that energy away from the black and whiteness of a win or a loss and evaluate and reward yourself or child based on a different set of criteria, you and they will, in turn, be more clutch.

Stop giving fear the power!

The way we talk to our children often becomes their inner-voice...use your words wisely. Are you creating fear in your child by how you speak to them before, during, or after a game?

Remember, we are not defined by our failure, but how we react to it (learn, grow, and improve). Losing the battle is not detrimental if your focus is on winning the war—having a macro perspective versus a micro perspective. The power of perspective changes everything.

Teach and model these lessons to your kids: Life is short. Celebrate the wins, learn from the losses. Adversity, obstacles, and challenges oftentimes are our greatest gifts. I don't enjoy losing, I just look at it differently. My self-efficacy can be found in the E & G columns (effort and growth), not by wins and losses.

So now my answer to the question "Do you love to win or hate to lose?"...

I LOVE TO WIN!

How can you infuse this approach with your team, family, and children?

CHAPTER 5

LIFE IS ABOUT CONNECTION

This past year on my birthday, I had a different perspective on how I wanted to celebrate. Like most years, my close family asked me what I wanted for a birthday present.

My younger self probably would have said, "Some new Jordans, clothes, a new gadget or piece of technology...," but as I've gotten older and wiser, I'm seeking what true happiness feels like. During my journey of self-discovery, I've learned that joy doesn't come from things, but from deep relationships.

And there's no relationship more important to me than the one I have with my amazing wife, Kendra. All I wanted for my birthday was to connect on a deeper level with my wife. Honestly, that's it. I'm not saying this to get brownie points, I truly meant it.

One of the best gifts you can give your child is to model a loving and caring adult relationship.

This sentiment brings me back to an epiphany I had while watching a TED Talk last summer. I was doing my best to multitask by checking out a few TED Talks on YouTube while watching the kids in our playroom

(I promise, Kendra, no one ate poop or swallowed Legos!), I stumbled across a speaker discussing a powerful insight into the human condition. He shared an eighty-year study from Harvard that looked into what brings happiness. Tracking 268 Harvard sophomores and their offspring since 1938, this study gave the researchers a wealth of data on what brings people true joy.

Through years of research, their conclusion: Connection and close relationships, more than money or fame, are what keep people happy throughout their lives.

"The surprising finding is that our relationships and how happy we are in our relationships has a powerful influence on our health," the director of the study, Robert Waldinger said. Waldinger is a psychiatrist at Massachusetts General Hospital and a professor of psychiatry at Harvard Medical School. "Taking care of your body is important, but tending to your relationships is a form of self-care too. That, I think, is the revelation."

If you are like I was for most of my life, where you look for status, things, money, accolades, and outcomes to bring happiness, then you will send yourself on a fruitless journey to a bottomless pit of emptiness.

Instead of titles and things, focus on people and relationships. You can't take things with you when you're gone from this earth. To live a glorious life, I believe we need to think about two L words: legacy and love. What kind of light did we shine, and what kind of wake did we leave behind...even if that light and that wake was designed for one person?

Let me ask you a question: What's the one relationship that is most important to you? Let's start there and capitalize on this amazing opportunity. It could be a friendship, your marriage, a parent-child relationship; it could be a mentor-mentee relationship. My challenge to you today is this: How can you make your most important relationship better?

This is kind of like how I used to shop for clothes. I used to buy many cheaper pieces of clothing that would not last very long, because the quality wasn't there. Now, I'm into buying fewer garments, but at a much higher price and quality. I now look for the one timeless piece that is worth investing in. *(Sorry, T. Do, you told me about the strategy a long time ago, but like most men I'm a slow learner.)*

What's more important to you, quantity or quality? I found that quality is more important than quantity.

Here are four keys to improve your most important relationship. If you do these four steps, I promise you, it will be the best gift you can give to yourself and someone special to you, including your child or children.

1. Love Yourself First.

This is cliché, but I often use this example to make a point. When there is extreme turbulence in an aircraft, the first thing flight attendants teach you to do is put the oxygen mask on yourself first, before you can help anybody else. How can you be of value to anybody else, if you don't have self-respect and love for yourself?

You have so much to offer someone. Forgive yourself. Love yourself. Accept who you truly are, and don't feel like you need to fit in. The goal is to belong...as in, belong to yourself first. Then you'll be ready to belong to somebody else.

2. Be Vulnerable.

To have ultimate courage, is to be vulnerable. I believe that the truest form of connection is to be authentic with others. Being able to share our pains, as well as our gains, takes a level of bravery. When was the last time you sat down with someone you truly care about and asked them what is on their heart? When was the last time you truly shared with somebody what is on your heart? Put the phones away and dig deep. You should never worry nor win alone.

Make today the day where you really open up to that one person that you care about the most (spouse or child). Invite them to do the same, and watch your relationship rise. I believe that trust is the ultimate superpower. If you have vulnerability and trust with another person, your heart and souls become stronger, healthier, and true joy is set free from our internal chains of jealousy, insecurity, and the lie of perfection.

Model this behavior, and your child will be more likely to talk to you when they are dealing with stress, success, and failure.

3. Be Intentional.

Greatness doesn't just appear. Whether you're an Olympic athlete or a successful entrepreneur, nothing ever happens by accident. Effort and persistence are the engine that drives achievement. I'll sometimes ask people in struggling relationships, "Are you putting in the same effort you did now as you did when you began the relationship?"

That's usually a wake-up call. I'm tired of the excuses "I'm so busy" or "We're so busy."

Stop that garbage. The phone call can wait. Answering that text message or email can wait. Stop lying to yourself and glorifying the hustle. Having a deep, loving, and committed relationship is much cooler than how many followers you have on Instagram or digits in your bank account.

Here's a thought: Schedule quality time in your calendar just like you would any other important meeting.

I promise you this, when you look back on your life, I'll bet that you'll yearn more for feelings, moments, and experiences with somebody you love, versus watching a TV show, sleeping, working seventy hours per week, or buying some random thing that you won't care about in a year.

Make some memories today, and do it with somebody you love.

4. Give More Than You Receive.

Kendra and I often discuss the power of giving and expecting nothing in return. That's the core mission of our marriage. We don't always execute this perfectly, but that is our intent. When giving and serving is the focus—whether you call it God or the universe—you will receive much more than you will focusing solely on yourself.

I think we just get lazy and lost in our own egos. We let pride stand in the way of our progress, as individuals and as a pair. Imagine if two people shared the common mission to truly serve the other person for the better. Picture what miracles and joy can be created with that mindset.

How can you serve your go-to person better? What's one thing you can do today that you know will fill their bucket? If this is the focus for each of you, you will experience the synergy of sacrifice and service. You both will rise to a fulfillment level way higher than when seeking your desires on your own.

Modeling this approach to your children is a game-changer and will increase the likelihood that they will serve others as well.

Happy Relationship Game Plan (do this today and watch your happiness and relationship RISE!):

1. Identify the relationship that is most important to you.

2. Tell yourself that you are amazing, that you are awesome just the way you are, and you have what it takes to bring value to the person you love the most.

3. Be intentional about scheduling quality time and doing something that you enjoy together with that person. But here's the twist, make that date or that event all about the other person, and see what happens.

4. Open up and be vulnerable about something that you don't normally talk about. Ask the other person to do the same.

This might be strange or uncomfortable for you, or you might be a pro at this. Either way, what do you have to lose?

For the record, my birthday with Kendra was amazing. While sitting down for pedicures together, I even let the stylists paint my toenails with the Seattle Seahawks "12" logo and a "K" for Kendra. Oh, the things we do for love. I was a little embarrassed at first, but then I realized that connecting and making memories with someone you care about is what life is all about.

After this experience, I took my four-year-old daughter, Bellamy, out on a similar date. The smile on her face was priceless. I believe by investing in her spirit and connecting with her on her level increases her sense of confidence and the most important stat in the stat sheet, her happiness.

CHAPTER 6

GRATITUDE AND CONFIDENCE

If you are a parent and have kids (especially young children), consider the following two concepts.

"Some habits are more important than others—the right habits have the power to transform your life."
- Charles Duhigg, *The Power of Habit*

"The type of emotional support that a child receives during the first three-and-a-half years has an effect on education, social life, and romantic relationships even twenty or thirty years later."
- K. Lee Raby, *Child Development*

Being a student of positive psychology, having a deep curiosity in human performance, and being a devoted father of four children ages six years and under, I'd like to share four simple activities that we do as a family in the attempt to shape their confidence, manners, and well-being.

By no means Kendra and I have everything figured out as parents—trust me, we fail a lot (is Paw Patrol a legal babysitter?). Nor are our children perfect angels. We have our fair share of tantrums and timeouts. However, with the aim to guide our kids to be their best selves, I'm going to share these family rituals centered around what are called "keystone habits." A keystone habit can spark chain reactions that help other good habits take hold.

Kendra and I hope these keystone habits will set off a cascade of more good for Baylor, Bellamy, Winnie, and baby Norah (prayers for sanity and sleep are welcome!).

1. Eat Meals Together as a Family

Eating together as a family around the table—especially dinner—may seem like a small act, but it has a huge impact.

As Charles Duhigg writes in *The Power of Habit*, "Families who habitually eat dinner together seem to raise children with better homework skills, higher grades, greater emotional control, and more confidence."

We make it a point to sit down together, put our phones away, turn the TV off, and pretend like it's the 1950s and talk. We 100 percent make this a consistent routine. Kendra cooks one meal for everyone—even our two-year-old Winnie is expected to eat what is served. No one can leave the table without asking permission to be excused.

This nightly habit helps our kids learn patience, discipline, and to expand their palates. These skills will serve them as they are older, and this definitely pays off when we eat outside our house or at a dinner date (packing different food for the kids is too much work for us!).

What are your family eating habits? Do you sit down

as a family?

2. Say "Thank You"

One of Kendra's and my non-negotiables as parents is to raise our children with manners. The two pillars of having sound manners are these two phrases: "Please" and "Thank you."

A fun way we model and encourage this behavior is what we call the "Thank You Cheer." While we are sitting down together as a family and our meal is served, whichever parent didn't prepare the food (which 95 percent of the time is me) leads this group activity of thankfulness.

This cheer was inspired by the "team breaks" I used to do as an athlete. After practice, we used to all put our hands in the middle of the huddle and all yell out the same word or phrase in unison.

When we are all sitting around the table as a family, we can't put our hands together as a group (#shortarms #cantreach). So each person puts one hand on top of their other hand, which signals they are ready to begin the cheer. Once all hands are in the correct position, on the count of three, we all lift our hands in the air and yell, "Thanks, Mom (or Dad)!"

This is a simple and fun interactive game that uses movement to practice the winning habit of simply saying "thank you." Oftentimes if I forget, either Baylor or Bellamy will put their hands on top of each other to signal the Thank You Cheer. Gotta love the accountability!

This is a fact that I know to be true: Manners go a

long way...especially saying these powerful words daily: "thank you."

How are you modeling and emphasizing manners to your children?

3. Praying Out Loud Before We Eat

Public speaking was a big fear of mine in my teens and as a young adult. I am not alone with this trepidation. National surveys show that more people fear giving a formal speech then death.

Knowing this, we've tried to help our kids practice public speaking at a young age, even something as simple as praying out loud.

I usually lead our family in prayer, but several times a week (and now it seems almost daily), we let Baylor and Bellamy take turns praying out loud before we eat. We have noticed over time that both have improved in choosing their words and speaking with more confidence. Bellamy is more of a natural and will even volunteer to pray when we have guests over (this makes me a proud daddy), but Baylor has made great strides as well. Months before, he wouldn't even participate, but after much practice, he now volunteers.

This routine serves three purposes:

• It helps our kids establish a pattern of giving thanks.
• It gives them a microdose of public speaking practice.
• It encourages them to connect spiritually.

We believe these are all great habits that one cannot

get enough of.

Can you think of other ways you can encourage your child to step outside of their comfort zone?

4. Happy Breakfast/Super Excited Dinner
One weekend last winter, our entire house got hit with the *Black Plague of Sickness*. It started with me, and I passed this gift to our whole family. It was nasty. I mean, stuff was coming out of every orifice.

This was Baylor's first time throwing up, and it really triggered what we call "Mr. Worry." That experience was quite traumatic for him, and he often would worry that it would come back again. The fear of getting sick even impacted his confidence and desire of going to school. Because of this we had several tearful drop-offs—especially when he overheard his teacher discussing with a parent about a student being sick. On this day, Kendra even had to go pick him up at school.

Recognizing this pattern, Kendra and I have developed several strategies to quiet Mr. Worry, including "Happy Breakfast" and "Super Excited Dinner" (I will discuss additional strategies in Chapter 8). Since I understand and am a firm believer in the powerful effects of starting your day off with gratitude (including writing in a gratitude journal, saying prayers, etc.), I created these games that the kids love. Because in the end, you can't be grateful and fearful in the same time.

How can you trick your kids into being grateful? Make a game out of it.

We all take turns going around the table sharing one

thing that makes us happy. After each person shares, we count to three and all at once pound our clenched hands into the table and say together, "Happy!" This act helps us focus on positive things and gets the day started on the right foot, especially for Baylor. This helps him, and our entire family, begin the day with a smile.

Once we circle back as a family at dinner, we go around the table and share what made us super excited from the day—it could be an activity, a game, a toy, or even a person. After each person's turn, we point our fingers in the air, twirl them around, then touch the table in a quiet almost whisper like voice and say, "Sssssssssssuuuper excited" (with a big emphasis on the "S").

These exercises foster communication, dialogue, and tend to quiet Mr Worry. Winnie usually says she is either happy or excited about Moana, but I love to hear what B and B come up with each day.

After doing this for several months now, the older kids usually lead this breakfast and dinner tradition. I'm proud to say that Baylor closed out that school year without any nerves when being dropped off at pre-school, and this year we haven't had any issues with Mr. Worry at school. A lot of this growth was his own doing, but I believe this daily habit played a significant role as well.

As mentioned, see Chapter 8 for more about Mr. Worry pertaining to anxiety and additional strategies for mitigating the negative effects.

No matter the age of your children, having a gratitude

practice and sharing small wins daily is an excellent habit to form that fosters self-actualization, confidence, and communication.

What are you doing to improve your child's mental well being, mainly regarding gratitude and reflecting on small wins?

Kendra and I are still learning each day as parents. We have our fair share of ups and downs. But we believe that investing in our children's development and character is like compound interest—the earlier and more we invest the greater the return for them in the future.

I hope these four rituals spark some fun and new habits for you and your family. Taking the time to love, model manners, and have fun as a family are the greatest investments of all.

CHAPTER 7

FIVE KILLERS OF PEAK PERFORMANCE

The biggest competition to achieving one's goals are not external forces. They live within each individual. A lack of self-awareness and self-sabotaging behaviors hinder execution a great deal more than from forces outside of one's internal control. This is especially true with young performers.

Based on my research in human performance, as well as reflecting on my athletic and business careers, I've created this list of the top five killers of peak performance.

1. EXTERNAL EXPECTATIONS

The highest achievers from Kobe to Oprah have an insane drive that is intrinsic and not extrinsic. If your child is performing to please someone, receive validation, or are seeking external accolades, their journey toward excellence will be short-lived.

External expectations = Internal stress

Help your child ask these questions: "What do I want?" and "Why am I doing this?"

If those answers guide them down a path that doesn't lead to their deepest desires and passion from within, its time to reassess their internal motivation.

2. FEAR OF OUTCOMES

The best things in life do not happen in the past or future, but in the present moment. A big hindrance and block of accessing a flow state (being in the zone) is obsessing over outcomes. I believe anticipation is a key element of high performance, but if the focus is outcome-based versus process-based (key habits and techniques), your child will increase their anxiety and stress. They will play the "what-if" game and run through made-up scenarios that you have no control over (for example: What will they think or how will I look?).

Also, the number one killer of creativity is fear of failure. The key is to help your athlete shift their emotional state to be more in the now. If you can have the mental command to ask yourself and your child: "**W**hat's **I**mportant **N**ow (**WIN**)?" you will be more likely to not only own the moment, but WIN the moment.

3. LACK OF CONSISTENT ROUTINES

Has your child identified specific habits they must execute regularly during the preparation and execution phases? Developing rituals that aid one's performance is a hallmark of consistent high achievement. I'm not talking about Obsessive Compulsive Disorder-type behaviors, I'm talking about mental and physical routines that are specific to one's ability and activates focus and rhythm.

If they do not have a specific process customized to their skills and personality, and they just "wing it," it will be very hard to duplicate or scale success. Also, developing consistent routines will help bring a level of comfort leading up to and during moments when it's time to perform. Finally, having systems in place helps avoid "decision fatigue," which means not wasting mental energy making trivial decisions.

If done right and together, your child will focus on the process and not the pressure, and they'll be able to perform as their true authentic self and not a shell of themselves who is either overcome by fear or a lack of preparation.

4. OVER FOCUS OF SELF

Think about your most stressful moments during times of performance. You most likely were obsessing and over-thinking about yourself. To access a flow state, there is an exit of self. Understanding one's vision, core values, and objectives are one thing, but if an athlete competes with the mentality that "all eyes are on me," it will be very difficult to relax and perform free of tension and tightness. These concepts all hold true when your child is performing.

Help your child understand that most people are more caught up in their own image and outcomes versus worrying about every move they make or word they say. Encourage them to practice stepping outside of their world and put themselves in someone else's shoes. Empathy is powerful. A simple way to help lower stress is to train one's brain and heart to deeply care about others, think about the audience, and mentally say, *I care about you, but I don't care what you think.*

My other favorite strategy to exit self is to serve others and be an exceptional teammate, co-worker, or classmate (whichever performance field your child is in). Service to others reduces stress and releases the happy chemicals dopamine and serotonin.

5. DISTRACTIONS

Have you and your child identified common distractions that pull your focus or energy away from completing your objectives? I call this "3PD" or the "Three Ps of Distraction":

• *People* – What people in your child's life (friends, teammates, or family) knock them off their game with negativity or lack of support? Try to identify the people in their circle or your circle that either add unwanted stress or behave in ways that hinder performance.

• *Phone* – In today's world, our smartphones are an extension of ourselves. Apps, social media, texts, and emails constantly vie for our attention. Identify the main functions in your phone that slow down yourself and your child's production. How can you limit these performance disctractions? Give yourself and your child a phone curfew.

• *Procrastination* – What does your child hate doing or avoid? The chains of procrastination are slow to form, but develop a tight hold that impedes execution. These patterns of procrastination keep us from not only performing at our best, but stunt our ability to improve. If you can teach your child to do what goal expert Brian Tracy calls "eat the frog early" (as in, do what you don't want to do first), you will help free them up to completing more tasks and unlocking more creativity.

Help your child do a self-assessment. Grab a sheet of paper and draw a line down the middle. On the left side of the page, have them identify the biggest distractions that hinder their performance. On the right side, come up with a plan to counter or substitute more productive behaviors when these distractors pop-up.

If you know the answers to a test, your ability to study and come up with a plan to execute vastly increases. This list above is similar. Help your child master their self-awareness and address these challenges. If they can overcome these performance killers, your child will be happier and more successful. Good luck!

CHAPTER 8

HELP YOUR CHILD DEAL WITH STRESS

What do you do when you see your child get nervous and stressed? Are you equipped to: a) Identify when they are having nervous thoughts and feelings? And b) Do you have the right tools to help?

Many parents might sometimes say statements like, "Oh, you're fine," or "It's no big deal."

As parents, we need to have a better plan than this. Kendra and I are working on our "Mr. Worry Tool Kit." As previously mentioned, we noticed that our five-year-old son, Baylor, deals with Mr. Worry weekly, and his younger sister, Bellamy, had a "worry episode" at pre-school that sparked Kendra and me to research strategies to help them.

Kids and Stress
According to the Child Mind Institute's 2015 *Children's Mental Health Report*, analyzing children and teens, "Anxiety and depression are treatable, but 80 percent of kids with a diagnosable anxiety disorder and 60 percent of kids with diagnosable depression are not getting treatment."

Anxiety disorders affect one in eight children. Research from the Anxiety and Depression Association of America shows that children with untreated anxiety disorders are at higher risk to perform poorly in school, miss out on important social experiences, and engage in substance abuse.

Anxiety is even more prevalent in teens. According to Scott Goldman, a licensed psychologist with the Sports Science Institute, "Nearly one in three adolescents in the United States (31.9 percent) meet criteria for an anxiety disorder. Of those, half begin experiencing their anxiety disorder by age six."

What Can You Do?
Below are four strategies (in addition to using gratitude as described in the previous chapter) that we have used to help our children quiet Mr. Worry.

1. Acknowledge the fear.

Fear breeds off of isolation. Instead of down-playing your child's worry, acknowledge it and sympathize with their feelings. No one should worry or win alone. Normalize their anxieties. For example, when Baylor says he is "going to miss Mommy" while at school, instead of telling him, "There's nothing to worry about," Kendra says, "I know bud, Mommy is going to miss you too. I don't like to be away from you either."

The lesson is that sometimes we have to do hard things, but if we can acknowledge the source, and work through it together, we will be better able to cope and overcome.

2. Expose them to concepts and strategies that speak their language.

I love education and personal development. Knowledge is power at any age. That is why Kendra and I expose our children to educational material that they enjoy. We love shows like Magical School Bus and Daniel Tiger, in which there is always a practical lesson that increases their knowledge or gives them a tool to use in real-life situations (for example, the phrase "use your words...use your words").

Other great resources we have seen be effective are books:

- *Parent Pep Talks: The Mental Skills Your Child Must Have to Succeed in School, Sports, and Life,* by Justin Su'a (great for teens)
- *Wilma Jean the Worry Machine,* by Julia Cook
- *I'm Not a Scaredy Cat,* by Thomas Nelson

And the guided meditation on YouTube called *The Worry Bus*, which we play for them at night before they go to sleep. These helpful mental lessons have inspired wise comments from our children including when Bellamy told me, "Daddy, worries are just in my brain...they are not outside or real." Or when Baylor said recently, "Mom, when I go to school today, I'm going to leave my worries in my backpack and hang them up outside my classroom...I won't bring them in with me."
[Insert me doing an ugly cry here!]

We can learn so much from children. These statements made me so proud.

3. Empower them to work through their fear.

One thing we've learned to be effective is to equip our

children with solutions or steps to deal with their worries. Instead of allowing the fear to grow and build by letting our irrational brain take over (we call these **"ANTs"**: **A**utomatic **N**egative **T**houghts), we have taught them to run through a checklist to help calm their nerves. Below is a checklist for Baylor when he is worried about going to school:

- Have you applied your brave oil? (This is what we call Baylor's "Valor" essential oil roller.)
- Will Bella be at school with you? (Yes.)
- Do you have something to give Ms. Mary? (Baylor loves to give his teacher a little treat or small gift.)
- Is there anybody sick in your class? (No. Baylor has a fear of getting sick after a bad norovirus episode last year.)
- Who do you want to play with at recess?
- Momma is here and will be back in just a few hours.

Being a high performance coach, I believe in the power of self-talk. What we say to ourselves is ten times more powerful than what anyone else can say to us, even with children. Knowing this, preemptively come up with what performance psychologists call an "if-then" plan, as in you already have a plan "if this happens" (for example, insert what causes worry), "then I'll do this" (insert the plan).

What areas in your life or your child's life do you need to come up with an if-then checklist to mitigate Mr. Worry?

4. Utilize professionals when necessary.

Kendra and I have an unfair advantage in this space. Kendra's mother has a master's degree in social work and is a licensed counselor. My dad has a PhD in psychology and is a clinical child psychologist. We have a village of mental health support to help us through our journey. You might not have this level of expertise at your immediate disposal. However, I'd encourage you to work with a professional when appropriate. Whether you seek counseling services through your child's school, your local church, or through a private therapist, mental health is just as important as physical health.

There is no shame in seeking guidance and support in this area of your child's development.

Kendra and I definitely do not have all the answers, and we have our fair share of ups and downs with attitude, not listening, and worry tears. However, we have committed to being proactive with our children's mental health and have seen the benefits firsthand.

What strategies have been successful in your parenting journey? Please share with others. It truly does take a village, and let's help raise the next generation to have self-awareness, humility, courage, and tools to deal with Mr. Worry (or whatever you might call it in your house!). These skillsets will have a huge impact as small children, when they are teens, and as adults.

CLOSING

The other day, Kendra sent me a moving video from YouTube by author and TED Talk Superstar, Simon Sinek. The topic of his speech was on a key characteristic of effective leadership. This bestselling author of *Leaders Eat Last* and *Start With Why* shared a concept that really resonated with me. According to Sinek, true leadership is about creating a "safe environment" for other people. When this type of leadership happens, he says it creates a powerful force for high performance in a team setting, which includes trust and cooperation.

I hope the content from this book will do just that—provide you with tools that you can utilize to create a safe environment for your child to discover, thrive in, and truly uncover what they are capable of. Your child needs to be able to trust you. And you must lead the charge regarding cooperation—filled with empathy, love, and listening. Fear-based motivation just simply will not work or last.

This trust and cooperation concept also deals with how you treat your child's coach. As I mentioned earlier in the book, 70 percent of youth athletes quit by the age of thirteen. I wonder what the percentage of coaches is who quit due to the stress, lack of respect, and constant second-guessing from parents. Your child can see how you treat their coach. How can you model a collaborative and supportive approach? Youth coaches are not getting paid. They will occasionally make mistakes, like all of us. If you have an issue, instead of making a scene, discuss it in private with the coach and seek to understand before you label and make accusations.

I totally understand the importance of protecting your child, but sometimes we cannot solve every problem and win every battle for them. Teach your child to respectfully speak up to the coach, to ask for feedback and learn what they need to do to improve and receive more playing time. This strategy invites opportunities for collaboration, ownership, and courage—all critical life skills.

The question I have been pondering as a parent is, "How can I better blend both the concepts of autonomy and accountability with my children?" You see, I am learning just like you. Let's experience this life-changing blessing of parenting not in a silo, but as a collective village.

I am going to fail sometimes as a parent...we all are. But like we expect out of our children, let's be open to feedback and be willing to learn and grow along the way as well. Because true happiness is found in relationships with those we love and through the joys of learning and growing.

Along this life journey of parenthood, I hope you do both—continue to grow in your relationship with your child, and improve your skillsets as a parent.

I believe in you. Now go believe in your child, and believe in yourself.

 @COLLINHENDERSON

 COLLIN HENDERSON

WWW.THECOLLINHENDERSON.COM

ABOUT THE AUTHOR

Collin Henderson is a peak performance coach in the fields of athletics, business, and academics. He is an author, speaker, sales trainer, and mental conditioning instructor for a plethora of professional and amateur athletes, as well as business professionals.

He received his undergraduate degree in sports management, with an emphasis in business, and his master's in education from Washington State University. He was a standout starter in football and baseball—in which he was a captain, Pac-12 champion, and Academic All-American.

He has spent over eleven years as an award-winning, top-ranked territory manager and sales trainer with two Fortune 500 medical sales companies.

Collin, his wife Kendra, and their four children live in the suburbs of Seattle, Washington.

Visit thecollinhenderson.com for more content, information, books, videos, and tools to improve your performance.

23034448R00044

Made in the USA
San Bernardino, CA
19 January 2019